Financial Freedom Series book 1

THE PASSIVE INCOME MYTH:

The secret to using what they don't tell you about passive income to gain financial freedom.

CALEB HILL

ISBN-10:152388696X
ISBN-13:9781523886968

DEDICATION

I am grateful to my family and friends who inspire and support me through each book I write. In particular I am grateful to Phil who nags me to complete each book when my interest is caught by another shiny object and the current project is forgotten. I am grateful to all the entrepreneurs who have inspired, educated and motivated me through the years. Without you this would be a distant dream. I am grateful to all the readers of books. Without you writers would suffer the agony of unread words. I am grateful to Amazon and Createspace for providing a platform where writers can express themselves without having to grovel at the doors of publishing houses who are overworked and uninterested.

CONTENTS

CONTENTS

1 WHY THERE IS NOTHING PASSIVE ABOUT EARNING MONEY ONLINE

Most passive income ideas consume lots of your time (which isn't very passive in my opinion) or require a substantial investment up front. That is why this book is named the passive income myth. What they don't tell you about passive income is simple. They don't tell you that there is nothing passive about it and they don't tell you that for each of the usual ideas that are peddled the majority of people will only make a small amount of income if anything. So what is different about this book? It was written to cover the same subjects in a different way.

In this book I will illustrate to you that none of these methods on their own work for most people in the way they are presented by most books. I tell it like it is and don't give you false promises of riches for virtually no work. If you are reading this book with the idea that you can do a little bit of work occasionally, invest a few dollars here and there and get rich, then you are reading the wrong book! Or maybe you are reading the right book, because in this book I will set you straight on the realities of making money online.

There are hundreds of books, courses and newsletters that will tell you how simple it is to make money writing e-books, or blogging, or Amazon FBA (their product selling branch), or having your own YouTube channel and they are right. It is simple. Often it is easy too if you have the required skills or the patience to acquire them, or the money to pay others to do it for you. But the reality is that only a few will ever make big money in any of these things. Why? Because those 'lucky' few put a lot of work and/or money into making their little corner of the internet a success.

So the question is... what does work? Why and how? Those are questions that this book will answer along with a few more questions you probably haven't even thought of yet. I've spent hundreds of hours over more than 8 years thinking about all sorts of ways to earn an income online. I have indeed made an income from my online endeavors, but I can honestly say that I have never made it big because of a lack of time and money which are the two resources you simply cannot manage without. Lack of commitment and inspiration added to the problem as well.

So what makes me an expert in this field if I am not up there with the high rollers? Well I have tried it all, learned from the ground up how to do each of the things that people generally tell you to do to make money online. I know the pitfalls, the heartache and the frustration. I also know what does work and why. I haven't just read it on a blog somewhere and regurgitated it in yet another elaborate squeeze page falsely marketed as a book.

What you need to know up front is that not everything will work for everyone. Why? Because not everyone has the resources to do it well for long enough to see a return on their investment. That is also true for me. I didn't have the time to put into blogging and all the things that one must do to make a blog a success long term. Although I did manage to make a modest income from a couple of blogs. I also didn't have the time or money to market my blogs properly, which meant that they were unable to compete with the big boys. But most of all I lacked the patience to see it through for the long haul and that is something you will need in bucket loads to be successful in this business.

The same is true for drop-shipping (which was limited more by my available income than anything else); YouTube, which suffered from lack of inspiration on my part; membership sites, which suffered greatly from lack of technical know-how in a period when the software was less available and more expensive. As for Kindle publishing, I was slow on the uptake for this, believing that any book worth publishing needed to be accepted by one of the big publishers. I am rapidly making up for that serious omission. Well, you get the idea by now.

So why am I now writing this book? Because, as I said I have tried it all and learned the dark side that no one talks about. But more importantly, I have retired from work due to a heart condition, so now I have time in abundance to work on those things I didn't have the time and patience for before ... and I have found that given the right approach and attitude, these things do work.

I am by no means rolling in money, but doing nicely, without having to worry about needing to work for a boss ever again. That doesn't mean I don't put in a lot of work, I do. Many hours a day in fact. However, I can sleep as late as I want, then go to my laptop and work in my PJ's if I don't have the energy to dress. I can even work in bed if I am having a really bad day.

Of course, I wrote this book to sell and make money. I am not crazy, there is a demand for books like this and I am not altruistic. I just took a long hard look at the niche and what wasn't being said and decided that was where I could contribute to greater effect. Essentially, I am putting all of my mistakes to work for you so you don't have to waste time and money finding out for yourself what does and doesn't work. I also try and help you to understand why things work the way they do. Once you understand that, you won't need anyone to tell you how to do it right, you will understand exactly what needs to be done for your own business in any situation.

I want to put things straight before we go on. This book is not specifically about blogging or writing e-books or running a YouTube channel or any of the other things I have already mentioned. I will look at each of the commonly touted online income ideas and examine what works and what doesn't and why. I won't go into huge detail about each one since the idea is to give you enough realistic information to help you decide where you want to focus your attention to get started. Then you can go and research further. Some of my other books go into a lot more detail because they focus on just one stream or idea. Of course you can also choose from, many of the other books and courses available on each subject. I hope that by being honest with you and providing value for money, you will choose to see what I have to say on each specific topic, but it is always your choice like anything in life.

So who is this book for? It is for people who want to learn the truth about so called passive income without all the hype and unrealistic expectations. It is for those who want a down to earth look at the realities of passive income and what can actually be done to beat the odds. It is for people who are willing to put in a lot of time and effort and stick with it for the long haul, because the reality is, most people won't make anything more than single figures for at least 3 months, maybe longer.

What things will we look at in this book? Well, I am limiting myself to things I have some real life experience in, so there may be income streams that I don't cover here. But the principles that you learn in this book will enable you to properly evaluate other options and see past the marketing hype to decide if it is something you can afford the time and money for. Also to see if it sufficiently interests you to stick with it for the long haul. I won't promise to make you rich from what you learn here, but I will promise you will learn enough to at least save yourself from making expensive mistakes. So this book will look at:

- E-books (fiction and non-fiction)
- Blogging
- Amazon FBA
- YouTube and Podcasts
- Udemy courses
- Membership sites & affiliate income
- Freelancing
- Things you might not have thought of

I will also talk to you in the next chapter about multi-threading, which I believe is the best way to ensure a decent (livable) income without working as a wage slave.

So having got the preliminaries out of the way, let's start by looking closely at the myth about passive income.

Passive income, according to Wikipedia, is "an income received on a regular basis, with little effort required to maintain it."

Some things can be considered true passive incomes, according to that definition and according to what most people expect when they think of passive income. Earnings on shares and other investments would most closely fit this bill. The downside of this is that you need to have a reasonable investment before you start earning enough money to live on. How many of us have that?

You might also consider earnings from rental properties in this category. Once again, however, you need substantial capital to begin in this market otherwise most of the income from rentals will go towards paying for your loans. The benefits are realized in many years when the property has increased considerably in value and the loan has dwindled to nothing. Good for retirement income, but not really something that is going to replace your job in the short term.

Most of the books on passive income that you will find on Amazon for $2.99 or less talk about blogging, Amazon FBA, YouTube videos and such. But such enterprises are nowhere near passive income and never will be. The only thing one can say about them is that one day if you put in a lot of work and/or money, you may be able to cut your wage slave hours by half. Maybe, if you are really lucky, skilled, dedicated and hardworking you will be able to leave paid employment completely and work in your own empire.

Please, don't ever think that you can do a bit of work to get it going and then sit back on the beach and relax as the dollars roll in. That is unrealistic and the main reason why the majority of people fail in their first year, resigning themselves to working as a wage slave until they die or retire, whichever comes first.

So if you are ready to put in several hours a day, cvcry day of the week, then you are ready to explore the world of self-directed income. Yes. Self-directed income is the term I have coined to cover what is commonly known as passive income. I think it more closely represents what these activities are really about don't you?

The best thing about self-directed income is that with the right equipment and resources you can earn while you are on the beach soaking up the sun and fresh air. Note that I didn't say lazing on the beach? Self-directed income does not allow you to laze, although you will still earn income while you do take time out to relax or sleep. Or work as a wage slave in the early phases.

As for an investment you get to decide whether that is money, time or both. In reality for most people it is both. They only really get to decide on the proportions of each. You can start this business in what is known as a **bootstrapping** model, that is, spending minimal amounts of money up front. But the down side of **bootstrapping** is what you don't invest in money you have to invest in time. Because I know that some of you will need to start up using **bootstrapping** methods I will include a **bootstrapping** section in each of the chapters that deal with a particular income stream.

Conversely, for those of you who work too many hours to count and are **time poor**, there are ways to do this using less time.

But it will cost you more. Therefore, I will also include a section called **Time Poor** for those of you who want to go the other route and outsource some (or most) of the work.

So for the **Bootstrappers**, the minimum investment you can get away with is about $5 a week. Of course the more you have, the better because this absolute minimum is going to make things really hard for you and take a very long time to improve your income. Realistically, I would want to start with at least $20 a week if that is possible. I will show you how the bootstrapping model works shortly.

For **time poor** readers, the minimum amount of time you can get away with is about 10 hours per week. Think of it as 2 hours per weeknight, or perhaps one hour every weeknight and a chunk of time sometime on the weekend. You might even need to use the weekend for all your time. The important thing is that you allocate time and stick with it.

For the rest of you, you can expect to invest somewhere in the region of $25 - $75 a week depending on what equipment and services you already have and which choices you make for income streams.

You will all need a computer or access to one, as well as internet access. For **Bootstrappers** this may mean using the local library or other public access computers. Your primary investment will be time. The money will be spent on purchasing computer time (if your region charges for it), purchasing a memory stick in the early phases and paying for some marketing in the later stages.

For **time-poor** readers, most of your time will be spent in research, briefing outsourced workers to do the jobs you ask of them and checking over the work that is sent to you. As you can probably guess, the rest of you will do a combination of these things depending on your choices.

Bootstrappers in particular may be limited at first in the choices you make because of lack of funds. That is why it is important to understand all of the income streams and methods fully before you make a choice. You could perhaps choose something you would not usually go for in order to generate a bit of income that you can invest back into other ideas. Now you understand nothing is free and passive income means work, money or both, let's move on to the first and most important concept, multi-threading.

2 TURNING SMALL INCOME STREAMS INTO A LIVABLE WAGE

In the last chapter, we talked about the myth of passive income and began to understand that the reality is you will need to invest time and money in varying amounts to realize any returns at all.

I am not going to promise that you will ever make even a passable income through the techniques I will show you. It would be impossible for me to guarantee that. The results will depend primarily on your motivation to work, ability to invest in your future and your understanding of multi-threading.

This is the most important concept of the whole book, and I am putting it up front so you can read the rest of the book with a thorough understanding of it since it is going to make the difference to your results.

Many people go into the online business in one way or another because they see a high flyer who makes six figures a year and hope to replicate them. What they don't see is the hard work that goes on behind the scenes to make that income. A blogger like Darren Rowse (Pro-Blogger) or Chris Garret (Authority Blogger) don't earn high figures by sitting on their hands. No, they work tirelessly blogging, doing guest blogs, podcasts, attending functions, speaking and numerous other things to promote themselves and their blogs. They never stop, well perhaps for holidays and such, but believe me they work harder than many people do at their wage slave jobs. For most of us, however, even if we put in the same effort and hours, we are not going to make it as big as these guys.

Unless you are Stephen King or Ken Follet, you probably won't make five figures on a single novel either, no matter how well written it is. So what is the answer?

Multi-threading. At its simplest, multi-threading means to do the same thing many times over, or to do lots of different but closely related things. Or a combination of both. Now I know this sounds simple, and it is, but you might not understand why it is so effective.

The principles behind multithreading are threefold. First is multiplication. When you multiply a small income it becomes larger. So if you take e-books as an example. If you write one book and make $5 a month, that isn't really a good income is it? But if you write 10 books and make $5 a month each, suddenly you have $50 a month. Still not great, but definitely better than $5. If you add a website that also makes $10 a month in advertising, then you have $60 a month. I wouldn't advise you try to run 10 different websites unless you are completely insane or hyperactive. However, the concept of multithreading can be applied to websites and blogs in a different way which I will elaborate on later in the book.

Secondly, multithreading provides opportunities for cross promotion. If you write 10 books and have a website or blog, you can promote each of your books in the other books and on the website. Some of your readers may even start following your website and pick up new books as you release them.

Finally, multi-threading is necessary to take care of natural decay. In other words, things come and go in fashion. So if you are selling something on Amazon FBA for example, it will eventually go out of fashion. Therefore, you will need to be working on your next income stream before that happens and leaves you high and dry. The same is true for e-books. They have a life cycle. Releasing a new e-book can breathe life into your older ones as people notice you as an author. Conversely, people who bought your previous books and liked them are more likely to buy your new one as well. The new e-book will also give you a new income stream of its own.

The example I give of an e-book is very important because it is something you really need to understand. You cannot just write one or two e-books and hope to live for the rest of your life on the income from them. You need to be constantly writing the next book. The concept of multi-threading also means that you have to write quality books since no one is going to buy future releases if the first book they read from you is rubbish. The same goes for any of the other income streams. You have to give people value for money in order to stand out from the crowd and get loyal customers. So now you understand the basics of multi-threading, let's look at each section in a little more detail.

Multiplication.

This was explained simply in the introductory paragraphs, but I want to go into more detail to make sure you all understand this concept. This is what is going to turn you from another disappointed entrepreneur into a self-funded retiree. Okay, perhaps not technically a retiree, since you are going to have to keep working at this for years to come, but at least you can retire from your current paid job and choose your work hours and location.

So the basis of multiplication is that you do the same thing many times over to get the result you want. Or you do multiple things in order to get the result you want. Let's go back to the examples I gave before, but look at some realistic numbers. Let's say you wrote a Kindle book on productivity and it sold reasonably well. Say you sold it for $2.99 a copy and sold 5 a week. According to most books I have read on selling Kindle books, if you follow their marketing strategies you can easily sell about 5 books a day as long as your book is visible to customers and that means ranking well. My own experience matches that, but I don't like to generalize on my own experience since I don't have hundreds of books for sale. I have chosen a much lower figure of 5 books per week to show you that even with tiny sales this model will work in time. So let's assume that on average over time your book is going to sell 5 copies a week. Your profit before tax on that book would be $10.46 a week. I think that is doable for most of you if you follow the detailed instructions in the numerous how to books out there on the subject. For this example I am talking about non-fiction books. The average person would take say a month to six weeks to write and publish such a book. There are plenty of books out there that will show you how to do it in much less time, but I think realistically, if you allow yourself a month to get everything done well, you will have a profitable book that sells for years to come. As an example I wrote this book in about 3 weeks. It took me another 3 weeks to edit and prepare it for publishing. During the editing stage I began writing another book. I am also doing a PhD which takes up a lot of my time and attention. So if I can do it, so can you. If you are interested my book *The Kindle Profits Myth: The truth about writing for Kindle and how you can use it to gain financial freedom* is available to help.

In the first week you will sell hardly any unless you pre-market your book. But once it gets known a little you will sell well for a while before sales taper off. Such is the lifecycle of books.

So one book selling around 5 copies a week equals $10.46 per week royalties. But if you write one book per month, you can be earning an average of $125 a week after one year. Still not retirement income, yet but we are patient, we know that this thing will take time and next year those books will still be earning a bit while our new books are earning us more. Averaged down again that makes us $250 a week. Now we are starting to see some results. In addition, we have become more efficient at the writing and publishing process, so we have more time to either write more books, or run a blog where we can cross promote our books.

Please remember that these are very conservative figures, ones that anyone can manage with virtually no marketing knowledge. Many people do much better than this on each book. But this book is about exploring realities and I want you to understand the reality. Not every book will stay at the top of the charts forever.

To be realistic it is called the top 100 because only 100 books can sit there. Books can, of course, rank better in the top 100 charts that are specific to keywords, etc. However, no matter how you look at it there is only ever 100 books in each top 100 chart. With new books being written and released every day, this means realistically your books are not going to stay at the top of the charts forever.

The moral of the story is that multiplication in multi-threading only works if you are persistent, patient and productive.

Cross Promotion.

Marketing anything is best achieved by cross promotion, but you can't cross promote if you only have one item in your name. So this is the second aspect of multi-threading that will boost your income. This is also why I recommend you follow more than one thread instead of just writing many Kindle books for example.

If you write your books, and work hard on a blog that becomes averagely popular, you have a captive audience to promote your next book to. In addition, your book readers may come to your blog to see what else you have to say. Cross promotion is not just about marketing your stuff, it is also about marketing yourself.

If people know your name and like you, they will be more willing to buy from you. You have already broken one of the barriers to paying for your product because they know you. People instinctively trust those they know more than a complete unknown. So even if your primary income is through selling e-books, you should also have a blog which you contribute to regularly, in order to promote yourself and build trusting relationships.

Of course, these same techniques go for all other forms of income streaming that will be discussed in this book, I am just using these two as simple examples.

Natural Decay.

Nothing lasts forever. Book sales sky rocket only until a new one comes along and takes the limelight away from yours. Blog traffic comes and goes, fashions and trends change with the seasons. That is why multi-threading is important. If you just sit with your one reasonably successful blog and think you are going to be comfortable for the rest of your life, you are very mistaken. You should always be looking for the next thing you can work on, always be at the front of the new trend and always have something that can replace the income from the one thing you thought was going to last forever.

Fortunately, you understand the rules of multithreading and you have been working on a new book, a new blog post, a new market every week. You know what is going to trend next week or next month, you have already taken advantage of this month's trend, you know the ins and outs of the businesses you are in, so you can respond faster to the changing moods of your audience.

That is the real secret to multi-threading. To be on top of things and to always have something new in the wings being produced to take the place of those things which are tossed aside like Christmas wrapping paper.

For **Bootstrappers** this is harder because each thread will cost you money, so you may need to focus on something cheap to start with, like writing kindle books. But if you can put half of what you earn from your sales back into growing your business, soon you will be able to afford a blog of your own. Well, technically it is possible with little money, by using one of the free ones. But ultimately you want the control of your own blog with your own hosting. I honestly believe that the **Bootstrappers** are the bravest of the lot because they have so little and must give so much of themselves in order to succeed. But when they do it is glorious.

On the other hand t**ime poor** readers will find multi-threading challenging because it always takes more time than you anticipate. Even if you outsource everything you can, there will still be demands on your time for hiring, outlining, checking and such.

So we have talked about multi-threading and why it is important. I think that you all understand the basic concept enough now, so let's move on to looking at the first of the income threads, e-books. The reason I put this one first is because I believe it is the easiest for most people and it can be done with a minimum of cost which makes it ideal for **Bootstrappers.** It should also be something every one of you does as a sideline or as a backbone to underpin your other income threads.

3 A SIMPLE BACKBONE TO EARNING EVERY MONTH

This chapter discusses Kindle Books, but in reality it covers all the e-book platforms. The reason I chose Kindle is because it is the easiest for indie publishers (that's you and me) to make sales on.

I see a lot of Kindle books for sale at around the $2.99 mark and when I look at the number of pages I see there are 20 or 30 at the most. I know $2.99 is only a small amount to pay, but why would people pay that for something they could have had for free if they had gone to a blog dealing with the subject?

I also see a lot of negative reviews for some of these books. While everyone will get a negative review or two in their career, they are something you want to avoid if possible. People do read reviews before they make a purchasing choice and several negative reviews may turn them off if there are other books on the same subject with better reviews.

As I mentioned in the previous chapters, you want to cross promote and negative reading experiences are more likely to turn people off reading more of your work.

This chapter, like the ones that follow, is not a comprehensive guide to the topic of e-books. It is far too complex a subject to cover in one chapter of a book. The aim here is to give you some idea about the stream so you can decide whether to investigate further. I highly recommend you do since it is a viable stream for most people.

So e-books come in two primary varieties, fiction and non-fiction. Almost everything you find these days on writing e-books, particularly the ones that claim to teach you how to write one in a few days, or to teach you how to make thousands a month in sales are written about non-fiction books. Personally, I have seen some horrible books come out of those books and courses, since they don't teach anyone how to actually write. What they do is teach you how to scrape up a bit of information and publish it. The main focus of those how-to books is marketing. Actually, I do recommend that you read one or two of them, since marketing is going to be an important activity for you once your book is written.

First, let's look at the truth about Kindle books (the same goes for the other e-book platforms, but I recommend Amazon, for first time indie authors because it is the easiest platform to publish and write for).

Amazon has a paying customer base of approximately 300 million people. From that customer base, 70% of sales goes to fiction books. Of that 70% about 50% goes to romance novels. If you take a look at the top 100 paid list at Amazon, you will find only 4 or 5 non-fiction books. You will also find that about half of the books in the top 100 are romance. Romance readers in particular buy books monthly at the very least. Some buy them weekly. So if you think you can write or learn to write romance give it a go.

Why are people advocating that you write non-fiction if fiction and romance is so popular? Because it is easier to write non-fiction. If you are not up to writing fiction, then I also recommend that you write non-fiction, although I write primarily fiction under pen names appropriate to the genre. The other thing of course is that it is much quicker to write a non-fiction book than a fiction. Having said that, an experienced author can crank out one romance novel a month fairly easily.

The take-home from this is if you are capable of writing good fiction, particularly romance, then try your hand at it. Your first book may not do too well, since romance readers are often fiercely loyal to authors and publishers. Mainly because they know they will get what they want from them. But some will give your book a try and slowly you will build your own following if you write well.

If you aren't capable of writing good fiction, then you should at least try non-fiction. Anyone who has successfully written a term paper can write non-fiction. It is essentially solving a need for information and that is what a lot of people are looking for. Don't, however, just go to a blog and swipe a couple of posts and think that will do for your book. Aside from its breaching copyright, it will annoy your readers who will soon learn that the information they paid you for, was available for free with a quick Google search. You need to be prepared to do quite a bit of research, to develop your voice as an author and to publish the best book you can on the subject.

Writing non-fiction starts with research. Even if you are an expert on a subject you will still need to do some research before you start. This is so you can make sure there is a market for your book before you put time and effort into it. To do this you will need internet access for at least an hour.

Bootstrappers, this is where your first investment comes in if you need to pay for internet time. First, you need to think about a few topics you have some knowledge on since you want to make the most of your time online. If you can borrow a friend's computer even better, but if you are stuck with paid public access computers, then unfortunately you are going to have to do it tough for a while. For those of you who have free access to a computer, then your first $5 will be spent on buying a memory stick. You will also need some paper and a pen/pencil if you don't have your own computer to work on.

Time-poor people should have a computer or access to one because you will need to do some initial research before you start spending on outsourcing the work. This is where your first 10 hours comes in. I will explain some of the additional research you will have to do in order to save time on writing later on in this chapter. For now the rest of the information is also relevant to you so don't skip it.

So your first task is to research the topic of your book. This is a vital task because it will strongly influence the number of sales you make. The first place you will do research is on Amazon itself.

Firstly, you will go to the Amazon web site and look under the top 100 paid and free books. Take note of what non-fiction books are there (if any) because they will give you a clue about which broad categories are selling right now.

Next, you will go to the Kindle non-fiction top 100 and have a look again at which categories are selling well now. You can tell this by the number of books on the topic listed in the top 100. Now, you may not want to write in any of those categories, but perhaps you can find one that is similar, or that fills a need.

If nothing there grabs your imagination, then list topics that you know something about. Do you play a sport? Or have a hobby? What do you do for a job? What books do you read? What things do you know how to do well? Any of these things can be meat for a book. It doesn't matter if there are plenty of books out there on that topic, there is always room for one more. You may have a unique perspective on the topic that no one else has written about yet. In fact, I would say that it is better to choose a category with plenty of books in since this means it is a widely searched category that sells well.

Next, pick out the top listed book in your chosen category and look at the book rank. You will find it about halfway down the listing with a whole lot of other information. It isn't hard to find if you look carefully. You want to see if the book ranks in the top 20,000 of all paid non-fiction books. If it is, it means this category is worth pursuing. If it is in the top 5,000 it means that the category you have chosen is one people are buying right now. If it is in the top 2,000 even better. Do this for 3 or 4 books in the category listing. Ideally, all of them should be in the top 20, 000 overall. If this is the case, then this is your category.

Now you want to find out what people want and haven't found yet. This will be your angle. To do this you go to the reviews and look at those who give a 3 or 4 star review. Read the reviews for clues about what they thought could have been better, or what was missing. Make sure you address these in your own book. Next, you search forums related to your niche for common questions. These are things you should answer in your book. You could even write a whole book answering one question if it is big enough.

So, now you have your category and some ideas for gaps that you can fill, you need to do some research on your topic. Do this even if you are an expert on the topic because you want to know what other people are writing about it. If you are writing the book yourself then you need to make detailed notes at this point. **Bootstrappers** in particular will find that this is your most time consuming part. If you are running out of computer time, make notes and then research books in the library. It's funny, I think that many people have forgotten that libraries are full of books with information in, now that Google solves all our problems for us. Really, libraries are a treasure house of information and free for you to read.

Time-poor people, researching is where you will spend at least half of your available time, since you need to provide an effective outline to any freelancer you are outsourcing the writing to. So make sure you spend the time wisely and make a decent outline for them to work from.

The next step is to arrange the information you have gathered into a logical format and begin to write your book. Remember, you are going to use the information as a guide and perhaps a backbone, but you have to actually write the book yourself (or have a freelancer write it for you). No copy and pasting here or you will lose out in the end. Multi-threading only works if you provide people with quality.

How long should your book be? Well, I have seen many suggestions ranging from just 3,000 words and up. To provide something worth the money you are charging you should aim for 8 – 10 chapters of between 5 and 10 pages each.

In print form one page equals about 250 words in 12 point. So you are looking at between 1250 and 2,500 words per chapter, times 8 – 10 chapters equals 10,000 to 25,000 words. Kindle calculates things a little differently. They count each page as 350 words approximately, so a 20,000 word document will be counted as about 58 pages.

Of course, many books and courses will tell you that 30 pages is enough, and I have seen books with good content at around 30 pages. I have also seen books of only 20 pages with very little actual content. One book spent 3 lines introducing every topic and three or more lines after the topic telling me what they had already told me. Now I know this is supposed to be the correct way to write an essay, but not when you do it for every paragraph. Particularly when each paragraph only contains 2 - 5 lines of content sandwiched between the introduction and conclusion lines. It was clear the author had snagged a few points off the internet or from another book and padded it up to make a short book.

People quickly recognize it as padding because you don't have anything to actually say. Let me tell you I was not happy when I bought that book and certainly would not buy from that author again. Please don't be one of those! It may take you a month or more to write 20,000 words, but your readers will love you for it and will come back for your next book. Really, it is not as much work as you think it will be. As an example, I write an average of 1500 words an hour on a subject I already have knowledge about. So for a 20, 000 word book it is less than 14 hours. Add to that research time and I have the first draft of a book in a long weekend. As a guide for you, this book is just over 20,000 words.

If you absolutely have to, you can cut your book down a bit to 15,000 or 10,000 words, but please don't cheat your readers. They look at how many pages are in a book and if they buy your book thinking that they have 50 pages of information to solve their problem, then you had better fill those 50 pages with information that does actually solve the problem. Having said that, many readers do prefer to read short informative books. The important point being that even a short book must contain useful information that fully answers the question the reader has.

For the **time-poor** or those of you who can't ever imagine having the skills to write a book, you can find someone to ghostwrite it for you. This is not a cheap route and will still take you some time since you need to be able to clearly tell your freelancer exactly what you want and how you want it presented. This is where the additional research I mentioned for **time-poor** people comes in. You will need to spend some time researching the best sources of ghostwriters, and researching through the freelancers on those sites for the best writer to fit your needs. As an example, some reasonable freelance writers can be found on Freelancer, Elance and Upwork. Fiverr writers are cheaper, but I would be suspicious of the quality. The poorer the quality of a freelancer's work the more work and/or money you will have to put in to bring it up to scratch.

The most important thing to ensure when hiring a ghostwriter is that you own all the rights to the work. You need to be clear that you want to publish the work under your own name and will not be paying any royalties to the writer outside of the original fee you pay them for the work. The other thing to be aware of is that you may not get the quality you are hoping for. Certainly you will have to read and edit the book carefully once it is written (or pay an editor to do this for you). If you do go with a ghostwriter please be aware that you get what you pay for and it isn't going to be cheap if you want quality.

One other option you could try is to get a cheap ghostwriter to make up a rough draft that you then improve upon. This may be a way of saving time if you really don't have enough time to actually write the whole thing. It is not something I have done personally since I like to write my own books, but you might want to give it a go and see how it works.

Once your book is written you should put it to bed for a few days and begin working on a new one. This way you gain some distance from it and will more easily see mistakes you have made. You should do this at least three times. I do it about 10 but I am a perfectionist and still get things wrong. Honestly, it is much easier to fix mistakes on an edit than to spot them in your proof and have to go away and redraft then upload again. Those of you who are **time-poor** should be extra vigilant at this point, particularly if you are paying someone to format your book since you will need to pay them to format it again once you fix the mistakes.

Once your book is ready and you are sure there is nothing else needs fixing you should ask someone to proofread it for you. You can use a freelancer to do this for you and I would recommend that, but you can also ask someone you know who has a reasonable knowledge of English. Your readers will forgive a few punctuation errors, but they won't forgive spelling errors in these days of spell checkers. Alternatively you can use a proof reading software program like Ginger or Grammarly. The only thing you need to be aware of is that these programs are not perfect so you need a good grasp of grammar in order to select which changes they recommend. They are best used as a catch all for things you might have missed rather than something to rely on if your grammar is not perfect.

Now is the time to format your book. This is a little more complicated, but with a bit of effort and reading you can do it yourself. As a side note here, if you want a print version of your book as well, I would format it for Createspace separately from Kindle. Each has a different way of formatting and you will give yourself needless headaches by trying to use one format for both. I did that for my first book and the Kindle version didn't look so good.

This leads me on to talking about Createspace and publishing. Since it costs you nothing other than a little bit of time for formatting, there is no good reason not to. Some readers like to have a hard copy, so why not give them the option? Aside from that, it always looks better if there is a choice between print and electronic versions. This by the way is another reason why you should write longer books. Create space has a minimum size for books which is currently (at the time of writing this book) 24 interior pages. That includes the title page and so forth. They also have rules about how many blank pages you can have in a book. So, let's assume that with the title page, an acknowledgement page and a couple of blank pages you have 20 pages of content. If you don't cheat by using a lot of white space and such you will need to write at least 5,000 words.

One other point I want to make here is that Amazon has a program called Matchbook. What this means is that if someone buys your print version, they can get the Kindle version at a cheaper price. You set the price you want to charge them. As most of you will have noticed, my Matchbook price is free. I think that if someone has gone to the trouble of ordering a print copy of my book they should be able to have the electronic version as well for nothing. Anyway, that is just my way of thinking. You are of course free to do whatever you wish for your own books.

Anyway, back to formatting and uploading your book. Amazon and Createspace provide comprehensive instructions which are easy to follow even for a first time publisher, so take advantage of the resources. They also offer templates for covers and print books to make it easy for you to format.

Formatting for the Kindle is a little more complicated, but still quite possible for you to do by yourself. For **Bootstrappers,** this will be the best option, so you can either follow the instructions on the KDP website (Kindle Direct Publishing... where you upload your book) or search the internet for more information.

For those who are **time-poor** you could find someone on Fiverr who will format the book for you for a reasonable price. Honestly, I would recommend Fiverr for jobs like this. The work will be done in no time and for little cost. I wouldn't expect to pay only $5 for such a job, but you will probably get away with around $30 - $40 for a 20,000 word book.

Your cover is the other thing that is needed to make your book complete and it. Createspace has templates that you can use if you are artistic and can use either Photoshop or Gimp.

Finally, you will need to market your book. This is a complex subject and best learned from a book that specializes in it. Once again, I will iterate that there are many resources online and in books that will help you to market your books. If you can afford it, I would recommend at least two from different authors because everyone has a different perspective on the subject and you will learn different things from every book you read. Alternatively, there are some very good Udemy courses out there that will explain the subject with video demonstrations. Marketing can be done for very little cost other than time, or it can be done for a reasonable cost and very little time. It is your choice.

4 THE SIMPLE WAY TO BOOST YOUR MONTHLY INCOME

As I explained in previous chapters, blogging is another essential thread in the multi-threading approach. It is through your blog that you can cross promote your books and other endeavors. While a blog is going to take you some time, there are some interesting ways that you can minimize it and still make money.

Personally, I believe that anyone who is in business for themselves should have at least one e-book and a blog as a minimum, no matter what other threads they use to make their main income.

Think about it. If you do something really well and make good money from doing it why not write a book about it? Having a book in print lends authority to your brand as well as giving you a little income on the side. Your blog reinforces your brand and gives more authority, besides being a place where people can go to get more information about you and your work.

Making money on a blog is a little different to selling e-books, although you can always sell your e-books from your blog as well. Your main sources of income from your blog will be from advertising of various kinds. The three primary types are paid banner advertising, AdSense and affiliate links.

Paid banner advertising.

This is where people who want to reach your target audience pay you to put a box or banner on your site permanently (well, for as long as they pay you to do so). This is the closest you will get to passive income since the only thing you need to do about it once you have the contract is to put the banner up and keep blogging in the way you normally do.

AdSense

This is where you place a block of advertisements from Google and get paid every time someone clicks through from the ad. It certainly won't make you a millionaire, but if you have a blog anyway, the small but regular trickle of income from AdSense is worth having, particularly since you don't need to do anything for it once you have placed the ad blocks.

Affiliate sales.

Many companies will pay affiliates (that is people like you and me who have a blog) to place advertisements for their products. The idea is that you get paid each time someone buys a product through an affiliate link on your blog. Amazon, for example, uses affiliate links, so your e-book could be listed on many sites around the world and each of those blog owners is actively advertising your e-book for free. Their payback comes when one of their readers clicks on the link and buys your book. Amazon pays you a royalty and pays the affiliate their commission. Everyone is happy.

For affiliate links like Amazon e-books you can just place an ad block on your blog and leave it to do its job. For other affiliate programs you might need to write up some posts every now and then and place the links in the text. So sometimes affiliate marketing can be a little more work. But since you are making blog posts anyway, why not make the occasional one that might bring you a nice little sum?

Sounds easy, doesn't it? Well essentially it is. The tricky part is in getting your blog noticed amongst the many millions of blogs out there. That is where marketing comes in and we will go into that a little further on in this chapter. First, I want to talk about how to have your own blog.

By far the easiest way to run your own blog if you have a small amount of cash to spend up front is to get your own domain and hosting, and install a WordPress theme. WordPress is designed for people with little technical knowledge and can be learned very easily. It is very intuitive, but if you really have no idea where to start there are many courses and websites that will teach you how to do it. Of course, there are even easier ways, using Blogger or the hosted WordPress site for example. Squidoo is another option, as is Webs. All of these sites and many more will allow you to put up your own little blog for no cost at all. The downside is that you can't put advertising on them because the company that hosts the sites puts ads on for themselves. So essentially they are making money from your work. But it is a way for **Bootstrappers**, who really can't find the $10 a month that hosting will cost, to get started. You can always put some inline affiliate links in your posts on these sites to try and make a little bit of money. You can certainly cross promote your e-books as well. That is why I recommend writing e-books as the first step for **Bootstrappers**.

So, you know that you should have a blog for cross promoting and authority and have decided to make one, but what should you blog about? Well the most logical step would be to blog about the same subject as your book. That way your readers will be interested in your cross promotions. So let's start with that. Make a blog about the same subject as your first book. Or about books in general, or if you choose to write children's books, then your blog should be about parenting (since parents are the ones who buy books for their children). For more information and a short example, please see the last chapter.

Great, now you have a blog. You should know what to write in your first few posts since you will use some of the material you researched for your book but didn't include. See? Time efficiency here. For **Bootstrappers** this will be important since you're spending a lot of time working on your research and writing. For the **time poor,** you may decide to outsource your blog post writing. In much the same way as you outsourced your e-book you can find a writer to make blog posts.

Blog posts are generally less than 750 words, unless you have a very newsy type blog, so you can probably get away with a $5 or $10 blog post from Fiverr.

For **Bootstrappers** in particular, or anyone who has the time, I saw a very clever idea by one Fiverr seller. She had a very successful blog and got people to pay her to write blog posts for them and put them on her blog with a link to their blog. Think about it. She has people paying her to write blog posts that she was going to write anyway for her OWN blog. The only real change she made was to attribute the posts to the customer. That is one smart lady. I liked her idea so much I am planning to borrow it. The trick is to have a blog that has enough traffic for people to want to pay you to do this. That brings us to marketing your blog.

There are many ways to market your blog and get more readers. Fiverr has improved the odds considerably for people who run blogs that might be of interest to a wide audience. You can find many Fiverr gigs that will list your website on their social media pages for a day or a few days depending on what you pay for. These gigs can result in an increase of traffic if the audiences are looking for the type of information you provide. I would certainly suggest that you at least try one or two gigs once you have enough content on your blog to make it worth people's time to visit.

Guest blogging is another way to get your blog in front of a larger audience. The idea is that you write an article for someone else's blog and they put it on their blog so their audience can read it. Of course you are allowed to put a link to your own blog in the post somewhere, sometimes more than once. So people who read your post and want to read more of your writing will go and look at your blog. The magical thing about this is that because good blogs stick around for years, people may see your guest post a few years after it was published and still follow the link to your blog. So it can be a source of unexpected traffic. For **Bootstrappers** guest blogging is probably the best and cheapest tactic for bringing traffic to your blog. For the **time poor** this strategy might be harder to manage. It is possible to outsource the actual writing of course, but your blog's reputation will rest on the results so it may cost you a decent amount to have a professional writer do it for you.

Paid advertising (ie paying to advertise your blog) of course will result in an increase in traffic, but you might find the results disappointing for the cost.

Social media is another excellent source of traffic. Places like Facebook and Twitter are great places to use as part of your traffic strategy. Using social media effectively is a complex subject and beyond the scope of this chapter, but there is plenty of information available in books and on the internet. I will say, however, that at the very least you should have a Facebook fan page linked to your blog.

Other strategies include using sites such as Reddit to post a short piece about your blog. More than 20 million users look at Reddit every day. That is not an audience to be ignored. Just make sure you read the rules of posting and don't spam or you will be booted off or at the very least voted down.

Forums are also good places to get noticed by people who have an interest in topics related to your blog. Again, make sure you understand the rules, preferably before you join up. There is no point spending time on a forum that won't let you place any links to your blog, even in your signature unless you are doing so for research. Also, don't make a pest of yourself spamming or you will soon find yourself pushed out.

The key point about blogging is that you need to post some worthwhile content regularly. At least once a week, preferably more often. Once people find your blog and like the content they will return to read more of what you write. They will stop visiting if there is no new content when they look. This is the death of a blog since your blogging income relies on traffic. For the most part your blogging income will also rely on traffic that is willing to click through an affiliate link or AdSense ad, at least until you build a big enough following that advertisers want to pay you to host one of their ads. So for you as a relatively new blogger, your income from blogging will rely on traffic, targeted traffic in particular. Blogging takes quite a while to begin showing any results. Expect to spend months on a blog before you see any benefit at all.

There are one or two things you may also do to boost income for your blog, but they will take more of your time, so consider them carefully before you do them. One method is to run competitions with a small entry fee. The prize, of course, will be a percentage of the entry fee, leaving the rest for you to profit from. Another way is to sell related merchandise from your blog, which will tie in with Amazon FBA. On that note, let's look at Amazon FBA as another thread for you to investigate.

5 SKYROCKET A SMALL INVESTMENT TO A HUGE REGULAR INCOME

Warning, you will need some money to invest up front for this income thread, so it may not be a viable first choice for **Bootstrappers**. So how much will you need upfront? It depends. As a minimum I would say $500 but without a few thousand you will find it hard to make a good income. What a low entry investment will do is give you a start so that when you have enough to invest in larger products with a bigger profit margin you already understand the process. For those of you with no money to invest at all, please read this section anyway, since it will give you a basis for future thought when you do have the money.

Why am I focusing on Amazon FBA and not talking about EBay or other drop shippers? There are a couple of reasons. First and most important is that Amazon will do pretty much all the work for you, so for those who are **time poor** but have money to invest this would be a good thread to begin with. Secondly, setting up shop with Amazon is easier, again saving you time. That is not to say other drop shipping systems don't work, they do, but you may need to invest more time, money or risk than you do with Amazon. Still, if you already have a business on EBay, by all means keep running it. The more threads you have, the better.

So what is so special about Amazon FBA? Simply that it is automated, scalable and sustainable. Amazon will take your orders, send them to the customer, handle the payments and enquiries and send you a cheque every fortnight. Your earning potential is from 30% to 50% of the retail price. So the only work you need to do is choose the product to sell, find a supplier and negotiate with them, then list the product on Amazon. There are a couple more steps, of course, but these are the basics that will get you started with your empire.

The best thing about Amazon FBA is that you can start small and build up over time as your income grows. It is also naturally multi-threaded since you won't be selling just one item through this method.

So first of all, let's look at an example taken from real life. The product is a child's toy and sells for $39.99. It costs $12.99 to buy and ship to Amazon and Amazon charge $9.29 for their profit and handling. This means each item sold makes $17.71. The product averages about 5 sales a day so the net income per week from this item is $619. Multiply that by 10 similar products and you can see how easily multithreading can increase your income. Let's be a little more conservative. Using the same profit, but only selling one item per day. That would mean you would make $123.97 a week or $531.30 a month. With 10 similarly priced items, all averaging the same sales you would be making $1239. 70 a week or $5313. 00 a month. I don't know about you, but I find that an easy sum to live on.

Of course, as I stated before, you need to invest money into this in order to make money and the smaller the amount you have to invest the smaller the return, like anything. But don't let this stop you from beginning your journey into FBA.

The only thing you do need to be aware of before you invest anything is that it will cost you either $39.95 a month or a minimum of $0.99 per order for Amazon to handle your product, plus their profit margin of 30% or more, plus warehousing costs and such. So if you are selling something for less than $5 a piece you might not make much money. It also means that you will need a larger amount of money up front than most people will tell you. So I advise you to be aware of hidden costs and make sure you have ferreted them all out before you commit your money to this. Having said this it is possible to begin with only $20. If you choose the right product and supplier.

Okay, so now you see that you can make money with FBA but it is going to cost you some money up front, let me give you a quick overview of what is involved in selling this way.

First, like blogs and e-books, you need to research the market. Find out what is currently selling well, what might be coming into fashion soon, and what is going out of fashion (because we don't want to be trying to sell things going out of fashion).

Again, like blogs and e-books, the best place to start your research is Amazon itself. Using the same techniques as you would for e-books. For example, checking the top 100 items for sale and the categories they are listed in, which will give you a better idea of what to investigate for your own sales.

Your e-book or blog might also give you ideas for items to sell. For example, if you have a blog and a book about fishing, then it would make sense to sell fishing gear through Amazon FBA as well. That way you can cross promote even more.

Having selected the type of item you want to sell, your next step would be to investigate sellers. The easiest place to find them is Alibaba. Simply go to the website and plug in general search terms for the item. For example, if you are planning to sell fishing related products you might search under fishing.

Once the listing appears you can browse it and click on items that catch your interest. Each product will list where it originates (ie who the supplier is and where they ship from). It will also list minimum amounts you need to buy up front. This is important if you have limited funds because you don't want to choose a product with a minimum order of 5,000 units when you can only afford 1,000. Fortunately, there are always new manufacturers on the site who want to build up their supply line and are willing to accept fewer orders up front. This is also good for testing a product before committing a large investment to it. There are other sites situated in the USA which are perhaps better, but less user friendly to begin with. You can find more details about them in any book or course about Amazon FBA.

Once you have found a product that you want to start selling, you would contact the supplier and negotiate terms. You should also investigate importation restrictions and costs at this stage if the item is coming from outside USA. This is important even if you live elsewhere in the world. Amazon US operates out of USA and is subject to USA importation rules and taxes, which means you will be subject to them too if you sell through Amazon USA. There are importation taxes to pay for most items, but the exact amount varies depending on the type of product and country of origin.

You will also need to supply your tax details to Amazon even if you reside outside of the USA. If the USA has a tax treaty with your country you won't need to pay tax in the USA they will report your taxable income to your own government. If you don't live in a country with a tax treaty you may have to pay tax in USA on what you earn. I am not a tax expert, so I would advise you to seek help in your own country with regards to taxation, accounting and legal matters.

Once you and the supplier have come to an agreement you should make a contract with them. Again, this may cost you more because of legal fees, but it is a necessary expense. I am not qualified in law and can't advise you on this other than to say there are example contracts available on the internet. However, a wise businessperson would always have a legal representative check them over. Especially if you live outside of the USA you should have a USA legal representative check over your contract.

Once you have organized your supply and contract, you will need to make payment. The safest way to do this is to use escrow since the money won't be released to the supplicr until thc goods arc dclivcrcd to Amazon and certified as correct. Again, escrow will cost you a little more and some suppliers don't use it. But it is worth the extra expense for peace of mind.

Now you can begin to list your product on Amazon. Their interface is fairly easy to follow and quite intuitive, but if you need more information on how to set up your account and list products there are plenty of good books and courses available on the subject.

The same goes for marketing. The principles are similar to marketing for e-books and blogs. Like book listings, Amazon uses rankings to place the most popular products in front of browsing customers. So if you understand the principles of getting ranked well for books, then you can use similar strategies for FBA goods. The main difference is that you won't be giving items away free because you still have to pay the supplier for them as well as Amazon for handling the order. Again, it is an in-depth subject that requires more than one chapter of a book to explain, so I would point you to one of the many good books on the subject. Of course you can cross promote as mentioned before and like e-books, once people buy from you and find you provide good quality, they will come back for more.

One other step that is optional, but excellent for improving your brand recognition, is what is known as private labelling gods. Many suppliers of goods will print up labels that brand the product to you. For example, if you bought some fishing tackle boxes from a supplier who agreed to private label it for you then your brand would be on the printed label or insert when the product arrived at the customer's door.

The key thing about private labelling is you need to decide on your own brand. You may have already done this with your blog or e-book. But if you haven't, then you will need to do it before you take this step. Again, there are many good books about branding available and some good professional artists who will help you to create your brand along with designing labels and logos for you. I would use somewhere like Elance for such jobs, but you might be lucky enough to find someone on Fiverr who does a good job for a reasonable price.

Another important thing about private labelling is it reinforces your brand and image thorough your books, blog, products and anything else you market. Your brand is your best marketing tool.

I have not included a **bootstrapped** section in this chapter because I really don't think this is something that

Bootstrappers should invest in until they already have a reasonable and reliable income from other threads. I do however recommend that you do two things. Firstly, think about branding and learn what you can about it so that you can begin to implement it into your blog and books. Secondly, while you can't list your own FBA products on your blog, because you don't have any yet, you can list products of others, via affiliate links.

Choose items that are good quality and consistent with your niche, then list them as if they were your own. By this I mean you place as much importance on these item listings as you would for your own. This way your readers get used to you having products listed that might be of use to them. You may even write a product review of some of the items you list. Readers often make purchasing choices based on a recommendation from someone they trust. You are going to be that person they trust because you are building brand loyalty. When you do have enough money to invest in your own FBA private label goods, you can switch your advertisements to your own products. You could also write a post about your new private label products and perhaps run a special promotion for your readers to help boost your product up the listings.

Unfortunately for the **time poor** this income stream is going to demand more time from you than you may have initially expected and it is hard to outsource the setup work. So you may need to make a choice between this and another stream in the first months.

.

6 ANOTHER WAY TO BRING IN HUNDREDS A MONTH

YouTube works in a similar way to blogging. Your content in this case is a video instead of blog posts and your advertising comes in the form of those annoying ads we all click away from as soon as the sign at the bottom says we can. The difference here is that advertisers will pay you each time their advertisement runs for a certain amount of time. That is why you normally can't click the ads away before 4 seconds.

Your YouTube videos can also be embedded into your blog for additional content or as your only source of content. In this way you can benefit from both your blog's advertising streams and your video income streams. The traffic can be two ways if done right. What I mean by this is that traffic from YouTube can click through to your blog from a link in the description and traffic from your blog can click through to YouTube to watch your video. While video that is embedded on a blog may be watched from your blog, some people prefer to watch videos on YouTube rather than on a blog. (Don't ask me why, I have no idea).

Podcasts work in a similar manner, although they are often spoken word rather than video. If regular, both podcasts and embedded YouTube videos bring consistent visitors to your blog or YouTube channel looking for the next edition.

The value of both YouTube and podcasts is that you can pretty much duplicate content. If you have an e-book for example, you could publish it as a series of videos and/or podcasts for those people who prefer to watch or listen rather than read. Again, this is something all of you should consider because you are making use of the same material for different markets and thereby enhancing your income. You will find that YouTube appeals to some people more than books while others prefer to have a book to refer to.

Instructional videos are popular on YouTube because they can show step by step how to do things. Once you get a following on YouTube people will view your new videos because they liked your previous content. That is why it is important to ensure that your YouTube content is top notch. If you are not confident being on camera you can find an artist to create animations for you. Alternatively, you could create a PowerPoint presentation or use screen capture to demonstrate things on your computer. You can hire a freelancer to do the voice-over if you are not confident with speaking at all.

Podcasts are commonly on a recurring theme that people come to your site to view or listen to. The primary difference between podcasts and YouTube is that podcasts are housed on a website or a podcast "station". YouTube videos, on the other hand, are housed on YouTube, but may also be listed and viewed from your website or from social media sites.

Podcasts don't always earn advertising income in the same way as YouTube does. Think of it this way... YouTube earns you a small amount of advertising income every time an advertisement is shown. At the very least advertisements are shown on YouTube at the beginning of a video when you monetize the video. But they can also be shown throughout the video. It is probably better not to do this unless the video is longer than 20 minutes or you will lose viewers early which YouTube can penalize you for in the rankings. Podcasts on the other hand, are used to attract traffic to your site so that visitors are exposed to your other content and on-site advertisements which they may click through. You may even have an audio podcast on your blog and a link to Video content on YouTube to improve your multi-threading.

Podcasts consumption reached 46 million in 2015, therefore it is a useful adjunct to your blog or website.

YouTube in particular can be used to extend your presence and exposure on the internet. Think about it this way. If you write a book about making cakes, you would want to support that with a blog on cake making, where you offer some affiliate links of products your readers might find useful. If you also produce a couple of videos of you making some of the cakes in the book, your readers are likely to watch those videos and earn you a small amount of advertising income. On the other hand someone who is searching YouTube for cake making videos may find your videos and watch them, then being interested in your recipes follow a link in the description field to either your blog or your book. It doesn't matter which link they follow because the blog will also have a link to your book and your book listing will have links to your YouTube channel and your blog. Do you see how multithreading works?

We can't all be the number one viewed channel on YouTube, or the number one blog, nor have the number one best seller book. We may only make a few hundred dollars a month from any one of these activities, but together they amount to a few thousand.

If you are not sure about your ability to make YouTube videos yourself, you can always hire someone from Fiverr to make some for you. Or better still you can use some of the creative commons material YouTube provides to make remixes related to your niche.

YouTube doesn't have to be a video. Many of the most popular channels only produce music with a still picture. So if you are a musician, or your kids or friends are, then how about giving them some exposure on YouTube and earn yourself some advertising income as well? If you don't want to be boring and just put up a still picture you can use some of the creative commons films to create a nice scenescape. There are plenty of films that show scenery and can be used to make a visually interesting montage to go along with the music.

My first experiences with YouTube were two music videos I made. They were visually very boring with just a still picture. They still got plenty of views, though, because they had music that people were looking for. My later videos use the creative commons footage on popular topics and were viewed in larger numbers as soon as they were published.

The art of making money on YouTube is to choose a topic that people are interested in watching. Your videos should be reasonably short (3 – 8 minutes), which means people will watch them through since they are not required to pay a lot of attention for long periods of time. Another factor in getting your videos viewed is to have excellent descriptions and titles so that people are intrigued and want to watch what you offer. Of course you shouldn't "game" the system by placing unrelated information in the description, but you could write your description well enough that it encompasses many topics that are relevant to your video. YouTube is essentially a huge search engine and being owned by Google, it uses some of the same algorithms to decide which videos to present when anyone does a keyword search. Of course their engines cannot identify the subject matter of your video, so they rely on the title, the description and the keywords that you place with the video when you publish it. One thing that they do that you should be aware of is they check every video that is monetized once it reaches 301 views to make sure that the description matches what the video is about and that they keywords fit. This is to prevent people from cheating the system and filling up the description and keyword sections with popular keywords that will increase the visibility of the video but are unrelated to the content of the video.

For **Bootstrappers** YouTube is an easy way to begin because it is completely free. If you use the creative commons videos available and remix them you don't even need a camera. All you need is time and a connection to the internet along with your YouTube account.

For the **time poor** it is harder. YouTube does take up time, so unless you can pay someone to make videos for you, it is going to cost you some time. From my experience it takes approximately an hour to make a video from creative commons videos. Then another half an hour to add music, title and description, advertising, etc. Since you want to be adding videos to your channel on a regular basis that means you will need to devote at least an hour and a half three or four times a week to making YouTube videos unless you can find someone to make them for you.

7 AN AUDIENCE OF OVER 5 MILLION WHO WANT TO PAY YOU FOR YOUR INFORMATION

This chapter is about Udemy courses, but in reality it relates to all online courses. Udemy certainly isn't the only place to find or sell online courses, but it seems to have the widest variety of courses. Other platforms tend to be niche related, often graphic design related. These platforms may be an ideal alternative or addition to Udemy if your niche fits. However, for this chapter I am focusing on Udemy because it is an easy platform for beginners to manage and Udemy itself already has a huge consumer base that you can tap into. Think about this... it has over 5 million students registered and more than 13 million course enrollments. This tells us that there are a lot of potential students on Udemy that we want to tap into. It also tells us that many students take more than one course. So it is a worthwhile market to enter even if there are others teaching in your niche. It doesn't matter because your voice, your approach will be unique to you. You teach the things that others don't, they teach things you don't, so students may take more than one course on a subject to get a broader point of view. I know I take more than one course on a subject in Udemy and I can tell you that I have never been disappointed in the course content. I have always learned something new from each course.

If you know enough about a subject to write an e-book about it, you have enough knowledge to produce an online course. If you write an outline of an e-book for a freelancer to write it for you, then you can use that outline as your outline for your course. Ideally, each video of the course will last for between 3 and 12 minutes. Any longer that that and you tend to lose people. Sometimes you may need to extend it out to 14 or 15 minutes if you are explaining a complex topic and it wouldn't make sense to stop part way through. If you record anything less that about 3 minutes your students have to keep moving on to the next video and each time there is a break you provide them with the opportunity to stop watching your course all together.

Why is it important to keep your audience engaged? If a student stops watching a course part way through and never goes back to it, they are less likely to enroll in any of your other courses since they will be more likely to remember that they didn't finish the course rather than what the course was about. Additionally, towards the end of your course is the place to mention other related courses that you run, or to introduce your book or related material. If your students don't make it that far in the course, then they are not going to see the additional material. However, if you put the material too early in the course you risk losing engagement as students either go looking for the additional material or feel that the course is only going to try and sell other stuff to them.

As mentioned at the beginning of this chapter, Udemy is not the only way of providing short video courses to students, but it is well known and respected as well as having an aggressive marketing strategy. Which means that there is a large pool of people likely to see your course and enroll in it. Once upon a time most video courses were privately sold via websites and squeeze pages. Those are the pages you may remember that tell you all the reasons why you need to take the course and give you lots of buy now buttons all through the copy. Some courses are still marketed that way. The biggest problem with this method is that it is hard to get the course in front of enough eyes unless you happen to already have a large mailing list or pay large sums to advertise your course.

The main difficulty new instructors will have with Udemy, is being seen amongst all the other courses teaching similar things. Eventually, through student ratings and such your course should gain a high rating and be shown near the top of the list of searches, but early on it may be hard to be seen. One technique for overcoming this is to offer your course very cheaply for a short time to get some students who will hopefully leave a good review. Another way that is more effective is to make a short introductory course that is offered for free. People will often cnroll in frcc courscs to tcst whcthcr thcy like the instructor and the material. At the end of the free course the instructor provides a discount voucher for one or more of their other courses. This strategy brings more paying customers to your other courses, albeit at a discount. However, since Udemy uses the number of students who have enrolled in a course along with positive reviews and ratings to decide which courses to display on the first page of their course listings it is beneficial in the long run to offer discounted courses to students in order to encourage enrollment.

Additionally Udemy runs promotions from time to time where instructors can opt in to offer their course at a large discount. This allows them to boost their student numbers which raise their ranking as well as being more fodder for word of mouth referrals. Then there is the option that Udemy offers to every instructor where they can message each student who has ever been enrolled in one of their courses in order to offer other courses, discounts, etc. This is an excellent way of promoting your new courses to students who already know you and your presentation style.

Of course, like YouTube, Amazon FBA and Kindle books, your title and description are vital to selling your Udemy course. It is the primary way to get the attention of potential students. If they are looking for a course in your niche and your description tells them exactly what benefits they will receive from doing your course, whilst the competing course has a dry factual title, which one do you think they will look more closely at first? Yes of course, yours.

The technique of pricing high, but selling low has some positives and some negatives. The obvious negative is that you are selling your course for a fraction of the price you want to earn from it. The positive to that, as already discussed, is that you get more students enrolled and this increases the visibility of the course. The reality is that many Udemy instructors sell the majority of their courses at a fraction of the list price.

The technique of pricing very high works best for instructors in this scenario because students perceive the course as being worth more. Think about it this way. If a course is listed at $299 but on sale for $10 while another course is listed at $20 but on sale for $10 which one has the higher perceived value in the sale? The $299 one, right? Does that mean that you are losing $289 each time a student enrolls in your course when it is on sale? No, because some of those students couldn't afford to pay $299 for the course anyway and would simply pass over it and opt for the one they can afford. Others may be able to afford the course, but choose the cheaper one anyway, or do as I do and wait for it to come on sale before buying.

So the reality is that while you will see many Udemy courses listed for hundreds of dollars, many of their students only paid a fraction of that price to take the course. This doesn't mean you won't make money from Udemy. Of course you will. You only have to create a course once, but it could potentially be sold a million times over. Remember your multi-threading strategy. This Udemy course is not your only source of income. It is part of your multi-threaded strategy to earn small amounts in multiple places and cross promote each to the other.

Speaking of multi-threading, another strategy related to Udemy courses should be to take one or two of your Udemy videos from a course and place them on to YouTube. Udemy allows instructors to use some of their lesson videos as free samples so students can get a feel for how you teach before buying your course. Those are ideal videos to put on YouTube as well, perhaps altered a little so they are not exact copies. Not only will you earn advertising income from people who watch the YouTube versions for very little extra work on your part, but you will also gain new students from those who want to know more. Alternatively, you could run a series of videos from your free course on YouTube with the same effects.

With your multi-threading strategy you aren't going to leave it as just one or two Udemy courses and some supporting YouTube videos are you? Of course not. The wise multi-threader will also have a book on the subject of their course. Remember that you are probably creating the course from your book in the first place. So promote the book to your Udemy students. Give them your blog site to go to so they can read more on the subject and of course they will also see your books listed there as well as any YouTube videos, podcasts and related items that you sell through Amazon FBA.

Like everything you do, of course, it is important to provide your students with quality, so they are eager to engage with your other threads and enroll in new courses you may make. Udemy helps people to enroll in courses by offering them a money back guarantee if they find the course is not valuable to them or if the course doesn't fulfil its promises.

That is another reason why you should always make sure you provide quality content and fulfil any promise you make in your title and description. You don't want to lose potential income because students ask for their money back.

Udemy is another area that is ideal for **Bootstrappers** since it cost you nothing to create a course. Well, that is not technically true. You will need access to a computer, some type of sound recording device and either a video camera or PowerPoint to make your presentations on. You may also need some form of screen capture software, but you could select free versions to get you started.

For the **time poor** you will need to create a script so that you can hire a voice over artist to speak for you. Of course your book writer can also create the script if you trust their skills enough. You can also hire someone to make a PowerPoint presentation to go with the script.

8 LITTLE ADDITIONS WHICH BOOST YOUR MONTHLY INCOME WITH NO EXTRA EFFORT

This chapter is about adding membership access to a blog and affiliate marketing. First of all, let's speak about affiliate marketing. I covered it briefly in the section on blogging, but would like to revisit it in a little more depth here. If you have a blog or website you should have monetized at least with some AdSense advertising. You may not yet be big enough for companies to pay you to permanently host their advertisements, but that doesn't matter because you are a multi-threader. You aren't trying to compete with the big guns in any one field. Instead, you earn regular small amounts from many places and earn more than enough to keep you from ever having to work for a boss again. But you do want to maximize your income potential from every thread. That is why it is important to understand and use affiliate marketing. In essence, affiliate marketing means that you advertise other people's products and earn a small commission every time someone buys one of their products. With some products you earn a larger amount, but only when someone buys the specific product by clicking through your link. In other cases you earn a commission whenever someone clicks through from your link and buys anything on the site.

The site I am talking about primarily is Amazon. Now many people associate Amazon only with books. You know, of course, that they sell anything and everything. This means that as an affiliate, you can sell whatever they have on their site and they will pay you a small commission each time someone clicks through from your blog.

The exciting thing about Amazon is that they will pay you a commission on anything that person buys from their site after they have clicked through from your blog, right up until they close their browser. What this means is that if they follow a link to a book, for example, then decide not to buy it, but instead buy another one you still get a commission on the sale. You don't get that with other affiliate marketing schemes.

The beauty of Amazon is that they have millions of products in almost every niche you can imagine, so there is no reason at all for you to ignore this income stream. The only work you will need to do is to sign up as an affiliate if you haven't already, search the Amazon store for appropriate items, get the affiliate link that Amazon provides for you and place that link onto your blog. Amazon is marvelous at providing a wide variety of links for you to choose from. You can choose a text only link or one with a graphic attached which clearly shows the product.

Why would you choose one over the other? Well of course you don't have to choose, you can use both. I do want to explain to you how you could use each of them so you can see it more clearly. Say your blog was about cooking and you wanted to recommend a particular spatula that you use because it is so good at cleaning the sides of the cake bowl, as well as being easy to clean. You could use the text link in your content by adding a hyperlink to the name of the spatula. For example.

Scrape the batter out of the bowl using your sparkle spatula.

Now the word sparkle spatula would be hyperlinked with your affiliate link to the product in the Amazon store. Of course you could also write something about the spatula to encourage people to buy it, but that would depend very much on the context of your story. I don't recommend spamming sales pitches through your blog, but if you were talking about useful kitchen tools, for example, you could include a review of the spatula... or even several and add links to each of them.

Having added an in-text hyperlink to your product, you could also add a picture link in your side bar so that those who want to finish reading your article before clicking on a link can find it easily instead of having to go back through the story to find the text link.

Always make sure you select that hyperlinks open in a new window. You don't want to lose your reader just because they clicked on a link.

There are of course many other companies that offer affiliate programs and often pay a higher commission than Amazon. If you find one or two that fit into your niche, then I recommend you use them as well as Amazon. I don't recommend that you ignore Amazon in favor of other, higher paying affiliate programs. This is because Amazon pays you for any other products that your reader buys after clicking through. So if you do add other affiliate links make sure they are in addition to at least one Amazon link.

Just as a note, affiliate marketing is also known as CPA marketing. There are some large companies that list many CPA or affiliate programs within their network. They are worth while investigating for non Amazon affiliate links. Please be aware, however, that those with the best affiliate programs will charge you to belong to their site. This may be a good way for **time poor** readers to go since they will find a large variety of good quality affiliate links in one spot. For the **Bootstrappers** however, the cost may be prohibitive. Since these companies change on a regular basis, I won't recommend any particular one. Instead, I suggest you do a Google search for CPA marketing. That way you will get the most current active ones listed on the first page of your search.

So now we have briefly discussed affiliate marketing we will move on to membership sites. These take a little more work to set up, but once the kinks are ironed out they should only cost you a couple of hours a week to administer.

You can set up a membership site as an add-on to your current blog or site. Or you can set it up as a stand alone site. A stand alone site might be easier to administer, but the difference is minimal. The basic premise of a membership site is that people pay a regular small membership fee to access your site or a section of your site. Usually this section has premium information that others are willing to pay for.

Membership sites can also be forums, although the paid membership model is less used in forums. There are, however, a couple of notable success stories in the field. Warrior forum is the first to come to mind. It has a free section and several paid sections. Warrior forum is probably the premier paid forum in the internet marketing and blogging niche. Another one that was very successful was ProBlogger but I am not sure if it still exists as a paid forum. There are some paid forums in craft niches and they tend to do well, particularly if they offer patterns or other free or cheap items related to the craft on a regular basis. You don't need to be the one offering the free or cheap items with this model. You charge other creators for a seller membership where they can advertise and sell their products as long as they also offer a "special deal" once a month to other paid members. You can also offer paid memberships to crafts people who will then be able to purchase the special deals from the vendors each month. The downside of paid forums is the amount of time they take in moderating and administrating. It is for this reason I don't recommend them unless you have plenty of time on your hands.

So the crux of paid sites or forums is that your members must get some benefit from paying you that they can't get outside your site. It is no good just doing the same old blog posts as others in your niche and hoping that people will pay you to belong. They won't. However, if your niche is a particular craft then you could easily have a paid section on your blog where you share premium patterns, ideas or videos about the craft.

The biggest difficulty with membership sites is setting them up in the first place. Often they require sophisticated software in order for them to run without too much input from you. WordPress offers some plugins that will do the job, but they still require some technical savvy to set up payments. The easiest method for accepting payments is via PayPal and it is the method I recommend since it can be easily and cheaply set up. For the **time poor** I recommend hiring someone with the technical skills to set the site up for you unless you happen to be a very technical person yourself. For **Bootstrappers** you will need to muddle along on your own or delay membership sites until you have enough income to pay someone to set it up for you. If you happen to be a technical person you may be able to set it all up by yourself, but for the technophobes amongst you it will have to wait for another day.

I want to talk a little bit about PLR products (private label rights) and paid membership sites. I often see these promoted. People join up with a paid site to get access to these PLR products that they can then place onto a membership site and charge for access to. I don't recommend you do this because PLR products are not exclusive to you. Therefore, others are charging people to access the same products. Now that doesn't mean you can't also do it. Of course competition is healthy and if you offer a wider range or better quality, then people will choose you over the competition. However, you will be pushing up hill to get members, especially if you are in the blogging or marketing niches. Most people in these niches are experienced and are members of the same primary source sites as you will be for PLR products.

For those of you who don't know what PLR products are I will explain. People produce video and e-books and sell them as private label rights. Now, contrary to what the name implies they are not private. They are available to anyone who wants to pay the price for them. What PLR rights does mean is that if you buy this product you can sell it again. In many cases you can even brand it as your own and alter the contents to make it unique. It all depends on the licensing that comes with the product.

There are several PLR sites that specialize in just selling PLR products to people who want to sell them on. I belong to one called IDplr which has some useful stuff on there, but nothing I have been tempted to share or sell. I mainly belong to it so I can keep an eye on new trends in e-books and perhaps download a few to look at the content. Sometimes they give me ideas for writing my own books. I advise you never to simply copy what is in PLR books and sell them as your own, but by all means use them as a guide or prompt. The main problem with sites that offer PLR products to bloggers who want to sell them on is that they either charge a membership fee and then offer limited or unlimited downloads or they charge you per download. Either way it will cost you money for an unlikely return. If you can, however, make money from it, good luck to you.

9 USING YOUR SKILLS TO WORK FOR YOURSELF INSTEAD OF FOR A BOSS

When I say using your skills to work for yourself I mean exactly that. Why work for someone who will pay you the minimum they have to when you can work for yourself and set your own pay rate? Why get up every morning, dress carefully and struggle with traffic or passenger congestion to travel to work? Wouldn't you rather get up at your own time and check your inbox, work on whatever job you currently have at the times you choose? Well, so would I and that is why I choose to work for myself.

But I am a nurse/doctor/secretary I hear you say. Or I work in a shop, or a restaurant, what could I do from home? Well, that is where some creativity comes in. Not all jobs are transferable to the home, but that doesn't mean you can't work from home. Using the techniques and methods already outlined in this book you can surely find something to do to earn money from home.

Let me give you an example. Perhaps you are a nurse, but you also enjoy writing books on the side. Your biggest problem, however, is that you can't think of a good topic to write about. Well, how about working as a freelancer? Write books for other people and let them pay you to do it in your own time. Maybe you are good with Photoshop or something similar. Why not use those skills to become a freelancer?

If you are a cook, then perhaps you could set up a little business cooking healthy meals that you deliver to people in their homes. You know, those people who work for a boss just like you once did. You could even pay someone to deliver them for you if you chose to. Or teach others how to cook in their own homes. I am sure there would be a market for that.

For those of you who work in a store, how about setting yourself up as a personal shopper? Or shop for a group of people who don't really have the time to do their own grocery shopping?

Can you see how many opportunities there are for people who are willing to think outside of the box and work on setting up their own little business?

There are many different opportunities for you to grasp and make your own. Becoming a freelancer is one of the best ways of making a little bit of income for yourself to free you from the burden of working full time for someone else. You can start small and only take the jobs you have time for and then cut back on your work hours when you have enough demand for your work. For people who are unfortunate enough to have lost their job and have no income, then offering your services as a freelancer could be the solution which means you never have to apply for a job again. It is particularly valuable for the over 50's who have very little chance of finding a new job.

If you are still lost for ideas you can find plenty online. If you take a look at Fiverr.com, for example, you can see what things other people are doing to make a bit of extra money. I am not necessarily suggesting that you can earn a good income just from Fiverr but it can give you ideas of things you might never have thought about. Try to look with an open mind and give something a try before dismissing it as unworkable. It will cost you nothing to put a gig up on Fiverr or to apply to a freelance site like Elance. This is an excellent stop gap for **Bootstrappers** who need some income before they can afford to invest in other ideas.

If you can play an instrument you could teach others how to play, or if you speak another language you could offer your services translating documents. You hopefully get the idea now and will take a step towards starting a new venture in freelancing to add another thread to your income stream.

This is probably less applicable to those who are **time-poor**, although I would ask that you don't immediately dismiss it. You may not be able to use this as a beginning strategy because of your lack of time, but you can bring it in later on as you begin to let go of the nine to five grind.

10 WRAPPING IT ALL UP

Hopefully by now you are beginning to understand how multi-threading works. I hope that you can also see that while the income from what you produce may continue to trickle in for years, it is by no means passive. You need to do quite a bit of work to establish and maintain your income streams. The important thing is to focus on one niche and look at every thread you can add to the same niche. Then when that niche is filled and you don't think you can add more to it, find another niche and repeat. Many of you will be happy to stay within your one niche because new ideas will keep coming to you month after month.

To illustrate my point further, I want to tell you a story about my sister. She is interested in handcrafts such as quilting and machine embroidery. One day she started to design digital patterns for herself because she couldn't find what she wanted elsewhere. Then she decided to offer those patters to other people for a few dollars each. Soon she had a following of people who loved her designs. That business grew enough over time to make her a nice little income on the side. She also wrote several articles for magazines, which she was paid for as well. Recently I suggested that she might use her knowledge to write an e-book or two on the subject. She could even make a series of seasonal e-books with patterns and ideas in them. Each of these will only bring in a small amount, but together they will bring in a larger amount to add to what she is already earning from her patterns. Like me, she is approaching retirement age and the ability to multi-thread within her niche is attractive to her for establishing a retirement income.

I suggested that perhaps she could also make some YouTube videos on beginning machine embroidery, choosing colors, machines and such. Properly monetized, they would also bring in some income as well as cross promoting her digital patterns for sale and her books. Of course it will be more work for her initially, but since she is making items for magazine articles anyway, why not make a book from similar items? Why not make YouTube videos as she designs and makes the articles? Why not use her blog to promote her book and YouTube videos, embed the videos even, instead of just selling digital patterns from a storefront on the blog? She could also create some Udemy courses on machine embroidery. A beginner course, perhaps and a more advanced one are things that come immediately to mind. She could look around at Amazon and find some products within her niche to offer for affiliate income as well. Perhaps some thread boxes or something to store fabrics in. Later, when her income is sufficient she could invest a portion of it in her own products that she would then offer for sale on Amazon and exchange the affiliate listings on her blog for listings to her own products. Technically her income is sufficient now, but I wanted to show you what was possible for someone starting out rather than just from the perspective of someone who is already established selling digital products.

As you can see from the example, multithreading doesn't mean you need to stick to one income stream. You can extend the work you are already doing on one stream to other streams and multiply your income. Your own multi threading strategy will depend on your work, family and income status.

Using one of the examples in an earlier chapter I would like to give you another illustration to further help you understand the concept of multi-threading.

So the example is fishing. Daniel likes to fish on his days off and is particularly fond of fly fishing. He decides on my advice to write a short book about the basics of fly fishing. He also makes a website about fishing in general and has a special section on fly fishing. He makes a forum about fly fishing and charges a small membership fee for access to a location finder which lists where the best results for fly fishing are happening each week.

Daniel's book sells well in the first few weeks and he writes another one on advanced fly fishing techniques. On his web site he adds his books via Amazon affiliate links, so not only does he earn a royalty for each book that is sold, he earns an affiliate income as well. He also lists some fishing tackle and boxes that he uses himself, again using affiliate links. He writes some articles comparing various fishing rods and within that he places links to more Amazon products with affiliate links. Because his readers can see he knows what he is talking about they are more likely to follow his links when they are looking for more fishing gear.

Next, Daniel makes some videos of how to make some fancy flies. He places the videos on YouTube and also embeds them into his web site. In the video listing on YouTube he places links to his books, his website and his FBA affiliate products.

As Daniel's income increases he sources products of his own and slowly replaces the products he is promoting for those that he is selling through Amazon FBA. He still uses affiliate links to boost his income a little more.

Daniel spends a lot of time on his forum and sees a need for more information about fly fishing vacations. He decides to write a guide book to fly fishing vacations in his home state. He also writes a short article on the subject from his book notes.

As his income grows, he invests money in taking vacations to other states and writes some reviews on his blog. He also collects all of the information and writes books about vacation spots in other states. He invests in a video camera as well and makes a travelogue video of each vacation spot he visits, placing these on YouTube and embedding them into his blog.

Wow. It has taken about two years and a lot of work, but now Daniel is so busy and his income is enough that he can give up his job and work at his fly fishing empire full time. At this time he decides that it is time to make a Udemy course about the intricacies of fly fishing. Can you see how successful someone can be just by following their hobby?

Each one of you will take a different path, but each of you will reap the rewards as long as you are persistent and conscientious. This strategy will not make you a millionaire overnight and will certainly take a lot more work than you were anticipating. However, with care and attention your income will slowly grow until you are able to release the reins of employment and be your own boss. In the more distant future you may even be able to throttle back a bit on your activities and still earn a decent income. That will be something only you can decide.

I can't guarantee you riches and leisure. All I can do is tell you the opportunities that are out there and how to weave many threads into an income stream that is more realistic than the get rich quick schemes you see everywhere. I guarantee that you will work hard and long and see very little profit for your work in the first three to six months, maybe even as long as a year. I also think that if you persist, you will eventually see results for your work.

Ideally, however, you will have read some more in depth books on each of the topics discussed in this book and choose your niche carefully so you won't have to re-evaluate or perhaps start over.

There are some excellent e-books on each of the topics discussed so I urge you to look at purchasing at least one on each topic so you understand them on a deeper level. Alternatively, there are some excellent Udemy courses on each of the subjects I have discussed.

I want to take a little moment to cover some things I didn't specifically cover in this book.

If you don't have a google account you should create one today. You will need it for almost everything this book suggests you do. You should also start your blog. This can be done as soon as you have decided on your niche and is an essential component of your multi-threading strategy. You will need to have a web site or blog in place before Google will approve your AdSense account since blog advertising as well as YouTube monetization relies on you having an approved Google AdSense account. You should also sign up for a Google AdSense account as soon as possible. The earlier you start the application process the sooner you can start to make money from your YouTube channel and blog. You will also need an Amazon account and a Createspace account. For the Amazon account, you will need to sign up for the KDP (publishing) account and for an affiliate account. When you are ready to begin selling on FBA you will also need a merchant account.

Make sure that you have a bank account that is easily accessed by PayPal, Google, Amazon and any other affiliate programs so they can deposit your money. You should also gather your tax details because you will need to submit them to KDP, Createspace and FBA before they will pay you. While I am on the subject if you don't already have a PayPal account, you should make one and verify it. Doing all of this up front will save you time when it comes to publishing your first book, listing your first product for FBA, placing your first affiliate ads and monetizing your first YouTube video. By creating a Google account and having it approved for AdSense you will gain access to some valuable keyword tools that you can use in your niche research, blog posts, book titles and descriptions and YouTube video descriptions and titles.

I look forward to sharing more of my experience with you as you read deeper into each topic. Please keep an eye out for my other books.

ABOUT THE AUTHOR

I use the name Celeb Hill as a pen name because I find it better to separate out books in each niche with a different pen name. This means my readers are not confused when they see a romance novel or a book on baking under the same name. I have spent many years learning and practicing the topics discussed in this book. I write from first hand experience and am enthusiastic about the idea of working from home. My greatest desire in life is for everyone who wishes it to find financial freedom by working for themselves. I was forced to find an alternative to working for a boss because of heart failure which meant I was no longer able to manage a job. Needing to earn an income I turned to the only other things I knew well, internet marketing and writing. This book is a result of several years of study and many hundreds of mistakes along the way. It is my sincere hope that you benefit from the knowledge this book imparts.

www.ingramcontent.com/pod-product-compliance
Lightning Source LLC
Chambersburg PA
CBHW060354190526
45169CB00002B/595